MW01281986

# LO___

# SUPPLY CHAIN

# MANAGEMENT

## IN MULTI-DOMAIN
## OPERATIONS

**BY**

**JOSEPH W. GRAHAM, Ph. D.,**
**BUSINESS ADMINISTRATION**

Founder of *The Black Chair Series*.

Today, he's the author of over 100 books/eBooks such as *Master The Art of Context Thinking, The 11 Golden Principles of Context Thinking, Sense & Respond: Thinking at a 24/7 Pace, Thinking Quadrant: How to Think on Your Feet Even When You're Sitting, Strategic Foresight*, and many others, published worldwide.

# COPYRIGHT

# TABLE OF CONTENTS

Introduction - 7

Chapter 1: AT THE CORE - CENTER OF GRAVITY - 39

Chapter 2: MULTI-DOMAIN TRIANGULATION OF CAPABILITIES - 52

Chapter 3: MULTI-DOMAIN TRIANGULATION EXECUTION - 70

About the Author - 149

How do you develop your thinking to fully understand logistics and supply chain management in a multi-domain environment? Imagine this, by desiring to be so by enhancing your thinking by using Multi-Domain Triangulation as a strategy of layered/ relational networked geometry/spatial projection of people and *fluid flow distribution* that allows exponential growth in flexibility, precision, and coordination to *anticipate* and be *creative* and *effective* in any environment. Believing this, by the time you finish this book, you'll know how to get started!

Use Multi-Domain Triangulation in any situation where you can be conscious of and track of everything about what's going on around you, that you can't be lost in your own world, and can anticipate and have a successful outcome by shaping and influencing conditions.

Many of you have gone through the conventional schools and might have a hard time imagining that you can learn from a short unconventional approach to learning from a book. Let me reassure you that you can learn from this book, defy logic, and begin to think, know, and understand at another level; improving your imaginative wisdom and brain power.

The mindset revealed in this book incorporates the secrets held by only a select few over the centuries – and will allow you to amass money and wealth because you will have a deep understanding of how things truly work.

# INTRODUCTION

When you read this book on Multi-Domain Triangulation, you made a choice that will cost you time and energy. Why did you choose this book? You might have been prompted or driven by the cover design or your life experiences may have led you to this book, which I think is one of the most valuable books you could read. That's right. On the pages that follow within this book, you may find the very answer you have been looking for your entire life. It can provide you the key insight you have been seeking for years or give your life a profound meaning for things you did not even know you wanted, perhaps your entire life.

In this book, which is a special book, I am going to answer your questions so you will easily know how I do my stuff, why, when, where, and anything else when it comes to insider stuff to developing the thinking brain power.

I should not reveal or share the secret knowledge told to me by a very successful person, but if you can count to 1, 2, 3...remember A, B, C, and maybe heard of the story of Black and White, you will see how easy it is to use these secret processes to make your life heightened, deeper, richer, and better.

These treasured secrets, uncovered in this great read, I will give you for free or for a fantastic small fee that only a small select few will take a chance to purchase this book. You are one of those Select Few. Use these secrets to build your personal library for successful deeper thinking and living. You will be able to discern the season and time to use your skills to educate, inform, advance understanding, and share knowledge. Once exposed to this knowledge, you will be changed with each reading as essential truths are revealed.

You can use this book however you want to, start at the beginning or jump around as you desire and just start reading. This book is designed to engage your mind and get you thinking, using prescience to see far ahead to new solutions, about developing thoughts and possibilities you might have never thought of before, like developing and training your eye to see details and taste, and stopping and thinking about what lies behind your perceptions of people, places, and things because your mind IS sharper than you think.

So, use this book carefully, it contains great secrets, shared over the centuries and it has come down to me and now to you. Don't let the secrets fall in the wrong hands, guard them and they will honor you with their staying power.

Now, the driving theme for this book is the question, **how to leverage Multi-Domain Triangulation at the cutting-edge of success?** We will answer that question in a profound way in this book. Multi-Domain Triangulation consists of three areas that will jump out at you at the right moment and that will be discussed throughout this book:

(1)     Think and Feel Outside-the-Box

(2)     Use Risk-taking on a Breath-taking scale based on priorities

(3)     Master of time, space, and mass (concentration)


This comprehensive book provides next-step insights for mastering the art of Multi-Domain Triangulation that allows one to anticipate and be resourceful in a given situation in any environment by gaining a deeper understanding of the relationships of capabilities that underpin things. You will be able to strike a rock and bring forth the hidden secrets within these sentences. I hope this book proves useful to several kinds of reader. This book focuses on on-going leader self-development to expand your thinking beyond your own experience and education to give you an enhanced, holistic look and broader, reflective perspective in time and space. It's an eye-opening, hands-on, look at how to master the aspects of the applications that go into anticipating circumstances and determining desired and successful outcomes. It will help you when you have too many different incoming signals interacting in unexpected ways causing growing problems. It will help you use mind bets to achieve results. Some beautiful insights and results will arrive with staggering suddenness, while others may take years to show up and be laid bare.

It is my goal to woo you and provide a compelling and revised way of thinking about how to increase strategic depth using exponential and spatial thinking that is happening as a result of converging exponential advances in technology. You can use the whole spectrum tools in this book to integrate and control any operating environment by learning how to use Multi-Domain Triangulation to sense how to know what to do next and why doing it is important to increase the velocity of resources across time, space, and function in the right amount, at the right place, using speed, connection, and access to information, while reducing risks.

Yes. I've used distributed logistics or distribution management, because it is what I know best to illustrate my point, and if you stay awake as I'm using my example, you will see the subtle, universal changes you are looking for. The business manager is unable to handle logistics due to disruptive supply chain cycle and complexities in supply chain intermediaries. Basically, logistics involve the distribution of goods from point of origin to point of destination. It is the practical art of moving armies and keeping them supplied. The assistance of transportation management will also be required to maintain lead-time from procurement of goods to end-customer delivery. So, my example using Multi-Domain Triangulation will show and give you the best expertise as it is relating to strategic and operational logistics and transportation planning management support within a field of supply chain management.

Let me advise you from the perspective of senior leaders, get a ring-side seat, so you will understand how to support mission needs with best practices to optimize your solutions.

I have designed this book in a way that you will learn about underpinnings of the levels of priority, domain, threat, power, and their significance and weights. The **three vertical triangulated dimensions and levels** that you will work with are on a *strategic, operational, or tactical level*.

You will be trying to determine when a shift or nuance on one level impacts or shifts actions on a new or another level. Domains are on a Physical level, Cognitive level, or Moral level (Is it ethical?) What are threats?

Are they a local, regional, or global threat? What are impacts the elements of National Power – Political, Military, Economic, Social, Intellectual, and Influence? What are the impacts of "DOTMLPF Spectrum" – which stands for "Doctrine, Organization, Training, Materiel, Leadership & Education, Personnel, and Facilities? What are the impacts of unknown or unanticipated inputs?

You will learn to take the three vertical levels and integrate them with **horizontal triangulated levels** (traditional linear thinking that uses **action – reaction – and counteraction** as the basis of *seeing, thinking about, and then doing things* to create reality). You will come to look for and see that there is no natural harmony and unity between the horizontal and vertical levels. You will have learned how to know where you are at a point in time…identifying **Multi-Domain Triangulation** and shifts in risks that require mitigation and friction points such as error, delays, misunderstandings. You will learn when good enough can defeat better and better can defeat superior depending on the skill and design.

I have explained as clearly as possible so you will get a current understanding and a **Sense of Operational Design:** a three area platform that empowers you to determine how far you can go, how fast you need to move within, and how long you need to sustain your distribution system to optimize performance. The three key areas are operational reach/depth (determines how far you need go), operational tempo/rate (determines how fast), and Operational Sustainment/Direction (determines how long you need to stay in an location and sustain supply and distribution systems). All three elements provide the planner with the sense of the operational design. The Operational design provides you with purpose, intention, and a desired outcome.

This book will allow you to master the following skills:

- See through and size-up different situations quickly and come to a single solution repeatedly

- Understand how the world will work and move in the next 2 – 25 years

- Learn how to strategically think deeply and widely to improve decision-making skills and shift your decision calculus

- Know form follows function

- Identify six rules of war and life that are fixed in all situations

- Learn the priority of the rules of war that must be followed for success

- Master getting the opposition to violate their rules or will

- Deal with growth while maintaining balance, confidence, and creativity

- How to ask questions, make good decisions, influence others, prioritize, and take risks

- Get an incremental edge needed to win in any environment

- Ask even better questions and reflect to make better decisions that lead to insight

- Handle and adapt to the speed and variety of changing environments

- Disconnect from the noise and sense deeply the decisive moment

- Use algorithms, data sets, indexes, and themes to see results

- In a machine-driven age driving by speed – use judgment, time, and perspective as your competitive edge

- Step back and think about time-tested sharper ideas and applications

- Expand your intellectual horizons by the power of suggestion

- How to master plan, delegate, recruit people, and report information

- Think Outside-The-Box in a multidisciplinary way exploring and intuiting the profound meaning of things

- Grasp principles and underlying processes and values at a glance

- Relate new problems to old solved problems over a range of situations

- Learn what something means and more specifically, what it means to you

The contents will help you gain a holistic understanding of the underpinnings of the planning art community; that they are part of a much larger, more complex chain with the goal of reduction or shrinking of time-distance between **Strategic Geometry/Locations and Lines of Communication**. These two points are the pillars of planning art and the sharper position. The common center that undergirds these pillars interests.

You will come to make sense of the global/international environment. Making sense means knowing production rates and movement rates at different levels and how to mitigate actions based upon identifying where the leader should focus based upon known and unforeseen consumption rates and requirements to close the gap by shifting resources, increasing or decreasing requirements, and/or working to quickly recover processes that undergird support requirements.

The contents of this book can also be used as an intellectual guide when you need to make necessary course corrections as you navigate by leveraging sharper and sensored-networks to help change objective foundations of concentrated thought; which is based on simple and proven mathematics like calculus and geometry. With what I'm about to share with you, you will be able to analyze and sort out what's important and interesting as you put things into context, see new insights, and anticipate trends as the leader of your organization.

Now, what are the key questions that you should be asking yourself and steps you should be looking for to achieve your goals and objectives?

Shortly, you will see in this book that you must be able lead your organization from the center position using center of gravity which is a continuous process throughout events. The center of gravity can change during the course of a tragic event and may not be apparent or readily discernible.

For example, just think, the dinosaur has long disappeared from the Earth, but the butterfly remains. What is the secret to its ability to sustain itself? I believe that when you understand the tools presented in this book, you can have a long successful personal and business life no matter the change that is around you.

In today's hectic world, it is essential for leaders to be able to confidently find out and communicate what to do as they adapt to quickly changing situations. This is by far the best practical book on achieving success in your thinking life as you respond to those chaotic and sharper situations.

**The smartest leaders of all times share <u>proven</u> systematic sequences they follow using Multi-Domain Triangulation that leads to mitigation strategies that leads to success.**

My ideas are future oriented and as such are 25 years ahead of the rest of the world. They solve problems by showing the guiding principles, requirements, capabilities, processes, and way ahead when you are thinking and planning projects of strategic, operational, and tactical significance using the thinking with a phased approach.

A key question one needs to ask is: What are the key <u>indicators</u> that I'm seeing that support decision points/actions/events/priorities by level and phases of operation and the execution rates of tasks?

We are now beginning to play the game of life in a sharper and exponential way. We have to learn to work together under new gold-plated, concentrated, modular, networked, sensored, scalable thought process that is presented in this simple and impactful book.

You must know how to successfully maneuvering between projects to gain insight into dynamic thought processes that will allow you to see indicators that show emerging requirements, delays, patterns, and trends.

Take a seat and learn some essential secrets of success – a collection of filters to make information into a network that has simple rules and how to use them.

Imagine this, you will awaken to an intelligent and invincible thinking that allows you to see how you can fly higher than an eagle and best navigate any chaotic environment, saving the valuable resource - **time**.

You will be able to find out what's important, determine a general direction, interpret metrics, and determine specific meaning in events. Sequencing is really about concentrated time management.

One can best navigate traditional and non-traditional environments by seeing and experiencing the big picture; knowing the overall strategic plan and direction and then be able to see the parallel decision points and weights of those points within daily requirements and actions. This will give you the concentrated awareness needed to ask, what is my sense of the situation and what's next? Am I doing the right things efficiently that will lead my organization to success with quickness, responsiveness, versatility, and adaptability?

Rare innovative and thinking people like, Einstein, Galileo, Michelangelo, Napoleon, and you already know that you must see what I call "Seeing the forest beyond the forest"; that is, be able to quickly see and imagine actions and impacts, *in real time*, of other entities upon your organization and you.

You must immediately respond with the right solution. Seeing the forest beyond the forest allows you the response time needed to get the right answer given a range of possibilities given locations and lines of communication.

For example, I've been writing books and books since 2001 and have seen that people's reading habits are declining; they say due to a lack of time. I used the concept of "seeing the forest beyond the forest" and applied it to publishing.

Since people say they don't have the time to read, I stepped back, concentrated, looked at other industries, and asked myself a simple and direct question; what can I do to help busy people create more time? What can I do to save readers hours of precious time and wasted dollars?

The answer came to me to publish an entire book on "One Page". It is similar to a summary, but with more information that can be used right away.

Here's an example at http://jgrahamenterprises.wix.com/onepag books

I could not have prepared the "One Page Books" without creatively seeing the forest beyond the forest. I successfully moved between the internal projects and projects of the other industries using what I discovered were best to create a new product. Imagine what it would be like if you applied this simple concept to what you are doing and see if you can come up with some breakthrough and beyond the forest outcomes.

Let me show you how to develop your ability to easily move between projects and integrate politics, economics, technology, justice, and social/religion so your efforts are amazingly successful.

Today I'm introducing key time-saving thinking concepts and tools that you can use to get the light-bulb to come on and stay on when learning to close gaps in your thinking.

This book is ultimately about **your thinking in time in environments that are within known contexts**, which you can use to have more success in your life. You can learn the art and science of central position thinking.

Principles, concepts, interests, and tools lay the foundation for your success on your journey from this moment forward. You will become way smarter than your friends, family members, and peers. The concepts and tools are very easy to use. You will be able to find immediate answers to questions that have time pressures attached to them.

Now Strategic Geometry and Lines of Communications determines figuring out how much stuff you should have at different places and times. This would be considered the main things that you want to accomplish. You would achieve these main things by sequencing products, services, and other things over time and space and developing your ability to think on your feet and multitask so that you can go farther, move faster, and stay longer supporting your interests.

You have to do a preparation of the environment; looking at terrain, lines of supply, locations of key roads, ports, units/people, and weather impacts.

You can use the central position to understand the mind of your opposition and force them to do things against its own rules of war and get off of their central position.

Thumb through this book and see the new and modern ideas presented.

We take a brief look at the balancing forces of diffusion of knowledge, center of gravity thinking, the impact of elements of national power, context thinking, and exponential thinking in mastering environments from the center of organizations; when you are not necessarily the leader of the organization, yet you are a leader within the organization.

What I'm about to show you is quite simple.

It's really simple.

Simplicity was one of Steve Job's principles when he developed products at Apple. As you continue to rush into your busy daily life doing multiple tasks, you need concepts and tools that can assist you in filtering through the vast amount of information that is being broadcasted. You desire to anticipate the right answer during the right time on problems that confront you.

You have to first establish the framework/foundation that allows you to integrate, sequence, and synchronize requirements, available capabilities, and see the processes that link the two. We will then show you how to use means available to you to see indicators that manifest as time-savings or power generation at decision points on your way to success.

This beautiful book will awaken you to the truth about those things that are around you, physical, intellectual, emotional, and spiritual, that can help you clearly see shades of meaning and Multi-Domain Triangulation possibilities in everyday events. They help you to see the scripts and beyond the scripts one uses to make life more agreeable or less worrisome about everyday life.

We want you to have the perfect answer to fit your immediate need and have the priceless tools handy to save you some precious time.

It is our goal to help make your thinking life measurably greater, sweeter, fuller, and richer.

Let's begin…

Sequence 1: You first **Ask** the most important questions at all times…
**Am I doing the right thing, things right, and where is the center or pillar, essential meaning, and purpose of what I'm seeing**?

The answer to these questions allows you to see linear, geometric, and now exponential and spatial relations /relationships that are key to your understanding and insight.  You will see the practical strategic lines, what's between and behind the lines (triggers and indicators), what is happening in the margins and gaps, and be able to talk to why things are important and why an action or principle works.

**Your goal will be to take advantage of every circumstance by understanding their meaning and interpretation as they occur or likely to occur. You do this by learning...**

How to master adapting to circumstances and determining successful outcomes by rethinking them at any given moment.

# AT THE CORE - CENTER OF GRAVITY 1

Triangulation To Master of Time, Space, and Mass (Concentration)

First things first. You must develop your leadership and thinking skills using the concept of center of gravity with the key information for your life or industry. You have to know what your centers are, and triggers and indicators that show your decision points and thinking vulnerabilities. This is done to solve current issues and protect yourself from a large amount of conflicting information that is being created by others to hide the real secret about how to obtain power of thinking. Center of Gravity is the essential ingredient that binds tools, processes, and systems you are using in your organization and life. It helps to reduce risk and unnecessary duplication of efforts.

Now, let's define **Center of Gravity** to get a common understanding. Claude Von Clausewitz, a leading authority on Center of Gravity, felt that center of gravity is the "concentration" or "hub" of power.

Your curiosity, imagination, and insight will allow you to read and judge what is the center point or the focal point. Then you look at how things are categorized or grouped around the point. This allows you to ask (1) if there is a natural balance of resources? (2) what is the weight (importance) of the various components and (3) will the foundations support those components?

In a nutshell, you have to concentrate on and see if the over-all picture and higher long-term advantages outweigh the short-term disadvantages and immediate short-term loss. You have to see value or worth, authorities, and rewards.

All situations in life adhere to center of gravity. You will see and sense harmony and balance of when you awakened to the center of gravity of things. The geniuses of old, like Bach, Picasso, Plato, and Van Gogh, knew this to be true, and now you know it too.

Next, what counts is determining who has the ability to get things done. After that; knowing and understanding a thing and its implications on your situation. If you can understand the basic message and execute the tasks and steps that are associated with them, then you will succeed in seeing and communicating what and who counts.

Ok. With that out of the way, let's begin.

Now the Center of Gravity for navigating between projects are in knowing what will get the results you want fastest and in the quality you desire. Those things will bring increase with them and bring added benefits to you. They are the foundation or core of getting what you want from your efforts.

Below are areas you must focus on. Ask yourself these questions and listen for the answers to master any organization or industry.

1) What is the absolutely essential information needed?

2) What are the implications and ramifications of what I'm seeing?

3) What's the difference, or shades of meaning, in implications and ramifications?

4) Who else needs to have or know about what I have in front of me?

These four questions provide a symphony of answers for mastery in any organization or industry when used in concert with a center of gravity.

Now, as an example, everyone should know about the distribution of wealth gap that exists in the world and its impact on them personally. Forces such as a nation's elements of power impact all of us.

Those geometric elements of power are a nation's *political, economic, technological, religious, and social institutions* that form the foundation of nations. Political deals with policy, economic deals with capital/income flow, technological deals with innovation, religious deals with moral standards and ethical values, and social deals with relationships among and between groups/classes.

All these elements of national power are *pillars* that impact the distribution of wealth or the lack there of. They are reasons for inequalities of wealth and income in countries around the world. To clearly see the impact of each element, you have to use the center of gravity to establish within yourself a point of view of things you are thinking about and seeing. You have to see the important aspects of how other people live and use the power generated from the elements and how to apply what you learn to everyday events.

It is not easy to see shades of meaning. Creatively seeing the shades of meaning obviously is not always easy. You have to experience things to truly know them. Reading what's presented here provides insight, but to truly know the material you have to take a look at your life and examine it to glean the wisdom from your life experiences. Examine your life to see the wisdom and insight that you already have.

For example, now, as you know, the distribution of wealth gap is increasing. Capital accumulation levels and rates are leading to further concentration of wealth into fewer hands; the One Percenters (1%).

They have been increasing the wealth gap because they know how to build real wealth.

Real wealth is what I call capital/income ratio and flow mastery on an individual and group level. They have used their access to information in research programs to increase their training and skill levels about the rest of society. Capital here means a number of investment instruments and real estate that they own.

Income means the amount of effort they put into bringing in an income from labor. We will talk about this later as we talk about Context Thinking, but for now you should be aware of this fact.

The Wealthy simply know how to make their money work for themselves by ensuring that their **rate of return on capital** *exceeds* **the rate of growth** of Gross Domestic Product (GDP) or rate of growth of output and income of the economy.

You too can do the same.

You can do it by using the tools in this book to first get a firm understanding of what is really going on around you; getting the big picture and then acting on what you see by using the balancing forces of increasing your knowledge and using technology as your prime forecasting drivers.

You should also join with upstart groups of like-minded individuals who get your learning curve in a vertical position that allows you to learn things quicker.

Groups like network marketing companies are prime examples. Get in one today. Look for upstarts as they will provide the quickest way for many of you. Find one that focuses on education and literacy because knowledge is power. Use this power as a means to close the wealth gap. The diffusion of knowledge and investment in some training or skills program is key to your overall productivity and personal and professional growth. It will allow you to catch-up with the rich by getting access to information and sharing knowledge.

In sum, Center of Gravity is most useful at the level as an analytical tool to focus the effort against the enemy's strength while designing campaigns and operations to assist in analyzing friendly and adversary sources of strength as well as weaknesses and vulnerabilities. This analysis of center of gravity is a continuous process throughout the operation because the centers of gravity can change during the course of an operation and may not be apparent or readily discernible. Identification of adversary centers of gravity require detailed knowledge and understanding of how opponents organize, fight, and make decisions as well as their physical and psychological strengths and weaknesses. You must constantly monitor and concentrate on events that will cause the centers of gravity to change and adjust your operations and actions accordingly in line with Multi-Domain Triangulation.

# MULTI-DOMAIN TRIANGULATION

## OF CAPABILITIES 2

Sequence 2: **Seek** the many connections/relationships and different ways (perspectives) by looking around you, paying attention to what you see, know, and do now and expect to see, know, do to influence the future.

We are all genius kids at heart and want to acquire deep smarts fast. We have been taught the principles of wisdom and context thinking since we were kids through our nursery rhymes. It is in your makeup called DNA. Multi-Domain Triangulation allows to you collect data and put it into groups of like-minded information. This group of data can then be examined to see what patterns develop. What you see that fits together. These individual pieces of data or indicators become information that you can use thinking to begin to start to make into good knowledge.

Use Context Thinking to show the strategic geometry and wisdom needed as you use knowledge to make wise decisions and develop into successes. This action provides you with the new Multi-Domain Triangulation tools to be successful in your thinking. It shows how even simple nursery rhymes reveal how to concentrate using context thinking and exponential thinking.

The following stories will provide you with an understanding of how to change your thinking and make you more confident in your choices.

The nursery rhyme, **Jack and Jill.**

*Jack and Jill went up the hill*
*To fetch a pail of water,*
*Jack fell down and broke his crown*
*And Jill came tumbling after.*

This is a truly amazing and powerful story, but what makes it amazing and powerful?

The key things that make it amazing and powerful are they tell you about the four steps of context thinking used to make you think well. The story can be used as an example for you to become amazing and powerful when you think in terms of what you want, look for (strategic foresight), understand now, and understand about your life.

Now Jack and Jill wanted to get some water so that they would not be thirsty or to cook some food so they could have a good life. They needed some water so they could know that their requirement for water was good. You will need to get water and other needed requirements to make your future good (strategic foresight). To make your future good, you have to see what is coming at you. You have to look both forward and backward (strategic hindsight) to get an understanding of what you see or what are the "REQUIREMENTS" for your life. Once you get the requirements, they help you with the whole problem of how to live life in a good way.

Now Jack and Jill went up the hill so they needed arms to carry the pails. Their arms represented that they needed the **"CAPABILITY"** or other people's capability to meet those **"REQUIREMENTS"** by understanding **"what"** the requirements were and **"who"** and **"where"** they are located to help you. The pail was designed to hold water and other things so they needed a strong pail built to last if they dropped it. The type of pail represents the **STANDARDS"** or value that guide Jack and Jill's goals in getting the water; the **"why"**.

Finally, Jack and Jill went up the hill that day to get water for that day. This represents the **"TIME"** factor it needs the most impact that is the **"when"** or "now" to know the desire in your life.

These four steps, **Requirements, Capabilities, Standards, and Timelines** can be used with purpose, intention, and a desired outcome to understand the way you think about anything in your life. Purpose points to requirements.  Intention points to Capabilities.  Desired outcome points to expectation about Standards and Time you want to accomplish a project.  You will use these steps to understand new information that comes at you. Know how to size up relationships by measure, number, and weight and apply results by improvising and taking calculated risks and leveraging capabilities. It will allow you to use all data into easy ways so that it can begin to make sense to you. Any new data can be understood by use of these steps.

Context provides the framework to whatever you want to do in life. Context is based on the scarcity of resources - time, space, energy, etc. Context has four steps that we will cover shortly, but let's get a sound understanding of facts and assumptions.

Facts and assumptions resulting from the analysis are measured against a sculptured framework of four questions;

(1) **what is** *required*,

(2) **what are your** *capability* **to meet the requirement,**

(3) **what are the** *standards* **that are adhered to, and**

(4) **what is the** *time* **needed to get it done?**

Facts are statements of known data concerning the situation.
Assumptions are unknown data concerning the situation.

Many people have a problem identifying facts or just ignore facts, as if they are drunk with wine, because they don't' know how to properly apply them in a specific situation.

You should focus on and paint a picture by saying or asking "so what" when you encounter a fact.

What you should expect is to challenge assumptions.

You say to yourself, here is a fact about my situation and what does this fact mean? Is the fact a cause or effect, what are the pros or cons, is it a general to a specific fact or specific to a general fact, is the factual relationship a numerical or historical context?

A fact is real whether it is known or unknown. If a fact is known, you can measure it. If it is unknown, you can measure it by use of statistical probability or estimation of what you think you would see or where it is supposed to be located, or it could be an assumption.

Assumptions are suppositions or unknowns about the current or future situation, which are assumed true in the absence of facts, and are required to continue planning and thinking about your situation.

Assumptions should not wish away capabilities or assume capabilities. Your biggest enemy will be the unknown and assumptions. All assumptions not validated or eliminated in planning and thinking become risks in execution.

This captures all that you currently know and don't know in one place about your situation.

Next, be careful to build the framework in which you will leverage and execute the tasks needed to make your life successful.

The framework gives you boundaries from which you will operate.

Here you determine what right looks like projected in a future timeframe. If you can't see in the future, you can't take action and execute your power when stepping out in strategic leadership.

Frameworks allow you to see the culture of and focus on key people by identifying tasks, deciding what's important and what to *measure* and how to *measure* it, and at what acceptable risk to determine if you need help to achieve your desired results.

The following is a **Four (4) Step Framework** for you to use as you go through the decision-making process. As part of the process, the three basic questions you should always be able to ask and answer are:

- Where are you currently located?
- Why are you there?
- When, to where, and in what sequence do you move to ensure continuous improvement?

Know that there must be a range of acceptable performance for each answer. In power attainment, most of the time, it is not an all or none situation. So when you ask questions, listen for the pain, desire, honor, and information that leads to understanding and specific answers that meet your purpose against the range of acceptable general answers.

Another example that reveals that we already know how to use these processes is shown by another nursery rhyme, *Goldilocks and The Three Bears*. It is a good example of the process of thinking better with Context Thinking. Goldilocks focused on the **Requirement** to find a comfortable seat and bed to rest. She tried out Papa Bear's chair,

Mother Bear's Chair, and Baby Bair's Chair and saw that each had its own **Capabilities** to hold her. She also tried Papa Bear, Mother Bear, and Baby Bear Beds. Each was made out of different material, why? So that it would stand up under the weight of Papa Bear, Mama Bear, and Baby Bear. They had to have a type of **Standard** or they would fall to pieces. They had to go give a level of comfort. She found the Baby Bear's was just right and fall asleep to rest then which shows the **Time** to rest was now.

Finally, the story of the *Three Little Pigs*, show that you can sometimes get the **standards** wrong as the three pigs each built their houses out of different materials, but two of the three did not build it to withstand the Big Bad Wolf. The three little pigs were all aware of the **requirements** needed to keep the wolf out, but they thought different about what would be needed, **capability**, to keep him out. So each pig made a different house of different strength. After the wolf blew down the first two pigs houses, the third pig's house was strong enough to keep the wolf out that day, which shows the **time**.

So, these nursery rhymes show that you already have the capability to use context thinking and have been taught them at as a child.

Use these simple steps to withstand the huffing and puffing of the Big Bad Wolf, find you a good place to rest when you get tired, and get you some needed water and food when you get thirsty in life.

Now always keep this in mind, these four steps of context thinking are based on your needs and wants at that particular time in your career and life, because you perceive things differently say when you were in your 20's versus your 50's.

In your 50s, you have sufficient mature understanding of faith, virtue, knowledge, temperance, patience, godliness, kindness, and love.

It is helpful to use *paired questioning* to get you through the process. You should be asking **"what and whom, where and when, and how and why"**.

These questions and steps can be used throughout your decision-making /problem-solving process to make the best decision about your situation. They will allow you to "Sense" or measure success, have a wide visibility: connectivity 24/7 with a global focus, "Control" events by having the right people and capabilities, shared awareness and processes, same standards of success, and to "Respond" to issues with rapid and precise response; with speed, reliability, visibility, and efficiency. These are all required for mastering your life and to help you increase your rate of return on capital and close wealth gaps that currently exists.

You can read more about context thinking in my book "Master the Art of Context Thinking. http://tinyurl.com/p3sw2q8

# MULTI-DOMAIN TRIANGULATION

## EXECUTION 3

Making the complex, not easier, but simpler.

Sequence 3: **Know:** Seeing the meaning of places, people, and things while grasping the grand drama requires imagination based on seeing levels and expectations.

Now that you have an understanding of Center of Gravity and Context Thinking, we can now sharpen your thinking by showing you how to use this new information to gain power for self and determine how to get things done when you are not "really" in charge of other organizations and agencies.

First, I define power as the ability to get things done. That ability is the "power hub" and it is supported by the pillars of politics, economics, technology, justice and social/religion.

From this hub, there extend the five pillars which make up the combined effect of power; which is the ability to get things done.

Each of the pillars represents a different function of power.

Critical to each function are the people who work there and their certifications/ training levels, their reach or influence, the equipment or tools that they use, the systems they put together to produce output, and the processes used to make the system work.

First and most important of these are the people. Of these people, there are select groups of people who have "real power"; they are the "go to" individuals who know how to frame and shape a battle Force Multiplier and make things happen for their organization. They risk-take on a breath-taking scaled when they have competing requirements and have to prioritize.

I witnessed this during my military career, when the U.S. Army would bring in a select group of people, usually Generals, to manage a military campaign. You could call them the "Dream Team". This Dream

Team is located within all successful organizations and must be searched out when you encounter each pillar that supports the Power Hub. We will talk about my lessons learned from this "Dream Team" that was assembled to launch the Iraqi War and my insight into their thinking and decision-making process.

Second, their reach or influence is important in getting things done. They have the, it seems, natural ability to move easily between Power Centers and make things happen by looking for the gravitational pull in organizations. They are swift to hear, slow to speak, and slow to wrath. They know systems inside and out and know all the people who make them go.

They understand how to work a room when they need information and migrate comfortably between the separate levels of business, government, and even the arts. They *integrate*, for example, Federal, State, and Local Governments and Commercial Entities into one fluid organization within their mind; getting a clear understanding of the Interagency processes. People on the different levels respect them. It is gained because they are honest, accessible individuals and communicative with others; plus they are not easily dismissed because of their knowledge of what right looks like.

They know the way and their actions
are done in love, as a guide.

They are able to dig into the guts and take
on tough issues and sensitive to see what is
subtly happening. They can do this because
they make wise decisions by *recognizing subtle
differences or indicators* that others do not.
They are able to take calculated risks, like
delegate certain tasks to others to do their
will, because they have learned from
experience when to take such risk based on
odds of success and trust.

In a nutshell, they are able to both think
and feel outside-the-box in the face of
battle or circumstances,

To master a new form of communication,
you must develop the ability to rapidly

learn techniques and master the right tools and questions.

- Learn to adapt to change by answering correctly the questions raised by changed conditions. How many forces do we need? Mission Command, Critical Events, Risks, Money needed, Legal (Authorities and Agreements) , Key Leader Engagements (KLEs) or Facilities and Forces, Access, Basing, and Influence ($F^2AB$-I).

- Combine historical identifiable trends in leadership and manpower quality as a point to start your analysis.

- Know about the struggle between the warrior and manager mentality - Efficiency versus Effectiveness debate.

When Generals guess wrong, they are adaptable and roll up their sleeves and do the tasks themselves, because they can rely on their savviness, if need be to outmaneuver and move around obstacles. They know the rules and when to bend them and break them. Artists like, Mozart, Newton, and Socrates are prime examples. As well as, Beethoven, Goethe, and Hemingway.

When it comes time to stay on issues, change gears and switch up actions, they are not afraid and you can count on them. They sometime pull strings that only they know how to pull.

Third, they know the equipment or tools that are central to each pillar or organization and how they were designed to work together to produce a certain result. Knowing the capabilities or specifications of equipment and tools allows them to understand how much they can do and help determine when outside help might be needed. They have keen insight into processes as well and how processes can be leveraged or mixed to build the greatest capacity to respond to ever-changing environments. They know how to work a system by recruiting and building teams, coalitions, networks, and clusters of the well-connected that support each other.

The key to their success is their empathic ability to ask the relevant and important questions within each pillar of power. This ability allows them to *play the game* well and get the deal done by determining the worth, authorities, and rewards associated with each pillar of power.

As you read this book, think about what a person of power does and says and you repeat it and know that you to have what they have; impact, influence, an ability to effect change by calling the shots, and a willingness to stand firm when they see wrong.

The experience gained from taking a center of gravity approach allows you to obtain confidence in your decisions and what you believe you are seeing. Most people only believe what they can see. **It is those who can see what they believe in and understand the processes that supports it before it becomes a reality are those that become really successful in life.** It allows you to establish a central point of view to clearly see the lines of thought /thinking that support events. It also lets you see the many sides or vantage points that are on the extremes of that line of thought/thinking that reaches out to the *width and depth of points of view.*

You can then use the strategies to see the many sides of issues. Sometimes the ideal solution will not equate to the optimal solution with respect to the overall plan. You will be able to see, infer, connect, and then make rapid conclusions about the issues before you that are relevant to your life.

What are the indications, impressions, suggestions, questions, symbols, imagery, or answers that you are getting from what you are now seeing, feeling, and hearing?

Next, what can you infer from what you see? Where in the news have you seen this or heard this before from experience or knowing? What do you already know about the information or have learned? What do you need to re-look about what you know?

You must know where to look and what to look for. You are looking for patterns so that you can make connections that allow you to see some degree of harmony or order over the short term, mid-term, and long term.

The next thing you want to do is connect with the information. What new things does it make you think about? What does it make you want to do, say, see, or write about? What human, things, plants, animals can best illustrate the new information that you are thinking about? *Use your imagination* and your five senses to connect the information gained from the news.

Finally, you want to conclude on the basis of having an understanding of the new information and integrating it within your decision-making process to determine the best course of action concerning the new insight.

What you need to do is elevate your critical thinking skills and be able to adjust your actions while you are in constant motion. You must determine your center of gravity for processes and organizations and be aware of when you are crossing an important decision point or in a decisive moment. You have to ask yourself:

What is the fixed base(s) of operations? What is the main objective point? Where is the forward line of troops, strategic fronts, and line of defense? What are your zones of and lines of operations? Where are your temporary strategic lines of communications? Where are your natural

and man-made obstacles? Where are your
geographic strategic points that you might
need to occupy? Where are your
intermediate bases of operations? What is
the strategic value of each location's
capability?

What are the strategic geometric directions
you are seeing from this new
understanding? What is the overall
movement of products/services? Is the
movement increasing or decreasing? What
position do you hold in the market? When
does that position reach peak production
or distribution? Are the key rates rising or
declining? What trends are you seeing? Is
cost increasing or decreasing? What
specific movements can you detect in the
distribution of products and services?

What relationships do you need to establish or relationships that need to be changed? Finally, what distribution processes and organizations are moving in the right direction and those that are not and need to change?

For example, in thinking, focused on distribution-based logistics, you will need to know the rules of thumb, guidelines or metrics you will use to get a sense of whether you are on track to achieve your expectations. You must be able to see what products and services you have purchased, what's in inventory, what is being maintained, what has been ordered and is in transit to you. You have to monitor how fast and what is the time that you will definitely have the product or service on-hand. From this sequence of data points, you will need to identify redundancies by integrating, enhancing, seeing, and synchronizing your planning and operating processes against buffers that will allow you to cover consumption and replenishment cycles, preventing distribution disruptions. These buffers are based on risk tolerance that mitigate risk without creating waste and overburdening the transportation system.

## Exponential Distribution and Sensing of Sharper Layers as Multi-Domain Triangulation

Wisdom will be developed by instinctively judging what right action to take, based on knowledge, insight, experience, common sense, and

**understanding to see things differently, more broadly, and deeply.**

Here's another good example of practical application of the thought processes discussed in this book. Now, National Military Strategy is built upon three pillars of being able to respond, able to shape, and able to prepare for future operations and emerging trends.

Generals are able to perform their missions that support all three of these pillars within distributed networks. These networks consist of four types: **Physical (concerned with Quantity, Capacity), Financial (concerned with the movement of money), Informational (concerned with systems data collection), and Communications** (concerned with linkage of systems/processes).

National Power is based upon Strategic Geometry of four pillars: political and diplomatic, economic, informational/technological, and military. By using each pillar, one can defeat obstacles whether they are on strategic, operational, or tactical in scope.

Generals use Multi-Domain Triangulation to link strategic design to tactics or objective to events. They do this by sequencing of objectives and events over time, space, and function. They instinctively know when they go beyond their

culmination point and adjust
resources to compensate as they
extend their operational reach.

Time, space, and function mean looking at
decision points, lines of communications,
culminating points, indirect approaches,
positional advantages and strategic
concentration of resources, and deception.
Generals use triangulation of Land, Sea,
Air, Space, Cyberspace in support of
operations using a layered/relational
networked geometry/spatial projection of
forces and fluid flow distribution that
allows exponential growth in flexibility,
precision, and coordination to adapt to any
environment.

They look for advantages and things that allow greater initiatives.

*Decision points* add significant advantages. They are the most critical points and objectives that allow the greatest flexibility and momentum. They are key to defeating or protecting a center of gravity. Usually, there are more decision points than there are resources to cover them. Decision points are usually geographic, such as a sea-lane, a town, airfield, or boundaries, airspace. They indicate a point at which one must determine the best use of available resources and weigh that use against risk.

*Lines of communication* defines the direction of resources to the obstacles.

They connect your resources from your base of operations to where the resources are needed on the ground.  In the future, you can expect the lines of communication to be supported over extended distances by disbursed small units.

*Culminating point* is that point when you overextend your resources and can no longer sufficiently continue the momentum. Generals keep an eye on that fact that distance decreases capacity and efficiencies past this point.

*The indirect approach* allows you to move from unexpected directions or times.

Generals are masters of *operational art and design*. The know how to achieve objectives by sequencing of operations and use of resources in phases, branches and sequels, sequential and simultaneous warfare, and precision logistics that is reliable, responsive, and agile.

Sequencing of operations is *the visualization* of what it takes to achieve the end result. You sequence objectives, decision points, culmination points, and priorities over time and space. You look at centers of gravity and culminating points to envision requirements for each branch or sequel. Sequencing is useful when determining phases of operations. Each phase of operations should lay the groundwork for future efforts. All tasks to be accomplished under each phase and why it is important for that task to be accomplished under a specific phase should be addressed.

Generals also visualize how requirements will be filled by branches or contingency plans use of resources. Visualization allows the Generals the ability to do the parallel planning and provides them more of a valuable resource – **time and speed**.

They are able to ask and find the answers to what is relevant and what is the meaning or implication of what I'm seeing? What is the optimal? Minimal requirement? What is the probability of this or that happening? What are the acceptable risks and the tensions that I am see because of that risk? Who else needs to know this information and should be involved in the decision-making? Who should be sitting at the table?

You need to be able to focus those key people by identifying tasks and subtasks, determining what is important and at what risk, and asking how can you facilitate the process?

Now, what you should not do is lose sight of the big picture, look only at short-term actions, or assume that you can use a fixed way to solve distribution management problems.

Generals use the Central Position and Indicator Thinking.

They gain a holistic understanding that they are part of a much larger, more complex supply chain with the goal of reduction or shrinking of time-distance between strategic geometry and lines of communication forces.

They make sense of the global environment: Making sense means knowing supply and movement rates at different levels of the logistics enterprise and how to mitigate actions based upon known and unforeseen requirements. These efforts allows for the reduction or shrinking of time-distance between

strategic geometry and lines of
communication forces.

They understand and ask, what is the
current distribution system in place based
on? They also attempt to define the
system:

Definition of Battlefield Distribution
System = what are the keywords that are
the interaction or the quality of the
interaction between Processes, Capabilities,
and End Users.

Key components needed to understand the
system are:
1 - Asset Visibility (What can I see in real-
time?)
2 - Environmental Factors (What may
influence actions/decisions?)

3 - Prediction of Future Capability to Move Items (Forecasting Requirements based on indicators)

The process starts with the End-User, next the process for tracking assets: for example in the Army, Global Combat Support System – Army (GCCS-A) Inventory Activities, next what capability is required to store supplies, what material handling equipment (MHE) is needed, and finally what transportation is required to move the supplies. All three components have their own internal and external environmental factors that contribute to delay within the system. These factors must be identified and understood by all within the system to achieve efficiency and effectiveness of the system.

By having visibility and an upgrade in truck technology/capabilities, MHE, and Radio Frequency Identification (RFID), one will be able to re-route items/trucks while on the move based on priorities/unanticipated events.

One could also use the latest Global Distribution Management Systems to assist with asset visibility.

Still one must look at the Environment (It consists of conditions, circumstances, and influences).

In the military, we look at the Political, Military, Economic, Social, Intellectual, and Technological elements. Key here is to determine priorities based upon supply and movement rates and communicating this so leaders can determine mitigation actions and still achieve success at some acceptable risk.

Acceptable risk must be assumed in three of the following areas:

  - Process – Command and Control, Reporting, Asset Visibility

  - Capability - Facilities and equipment needed to receive, store, move materials

  - End Users - generate requirements and indicators of their need


One must look at the links between internal and external relationships accounting for different information requirements at different levels over time....looking for similar rates/patterns that are revealed and seen as feedback loops or after action assessments.

Four-Step Process:

Key to understanding the Central Position and Indicator Thinking is a four-step process:

1. Identify and focus on the critical/most important tasks to success.
2. Explain why critical tasks are priority over other tasks.
3. Focus on decisions needed to make over phases.
4. Explain what conditions would exist at the end of each phase and at end-state. Backward plan on needs to achieve objectives by seeing the triggers and indicators that shows significant change to decision points.

The areas that do not change when planning in any environments are:

1. Location

2. Decision Points

3. Defense/Protection

4. Offense/Attack

5. Where can I apply Speed

6. Where can I apply
   Surprise/Deception

**Remember this because it is key:**

The driving issue/criteria is how much
**RISK** are you willing to accept?  That
is...Acceptable Risk. Examples of
criteria are your ability to **SEE** things,
**PRESSURES** on key lines of
communications, **DAMAGE** to
infrastructure, etc.

**Examples of triggers and indicators are those things that SIGNIFICANTLY change or affect mission outcome; adjustments to guidance, definitions, environmental, and approaches, and of course, adjustments to timing.**

More than ever, you must seek next level simplification - simplification in technology, distribution management, and in driving efficient order out of chaos. Simplicity starts with powerful yet flexible knowledge that makes it faster and easier for you to see real time solutions to problems. You will focus on the distribution systems rates and levels that increases efficiencies and thus reduce delays and increases customer satisfaction.

In a world where thinking and technology are growing exponentially, the wrong distribution system bogging down by delays means your problems aren't being efficiently solved. Reliability, response time, and scalability matter. Time is money— slow response times mean less customer satisfaction and efficiency. With 100% visibility and the fastest response times in your industry, you maximize your time-delivery. Plus, you get real-time updates with no delay.

Indicator Thinking provides complete visibility into your logistics data, allowing you to monitor performance, act on insights and drive effective distribution strategies.

## Key Features of the Central Position and Multi-Domain Triangulation Include:

**Sense of Operational Design:** a three area platform that empowers you determine how far you can go, how fast you need to move within, and how long you need to sustain your distribution system to optimize performance. The key areas are operational reach/depth (determines how far you need go), operational tempo/rate (determines how fast), and Operational Sustainment /Direction (determines how long you need to stay in a location and sustain supply and distribution systems). All three elements provide the planner with the sense of the operational design.

**Framework Design:** Uncover rich, powerful guiding principles, goals, and conceptual underpinnings that deliver business-critical insight in seconds. Potential inputs to guiding principles could be CEO directives and who does he need to influence to move the company to success. Goals can be made by taking time to visualize what ends the CEO wants. Conceptual underpinnings that must be address in any planning effort would be the number of people needed, equipment readiness rates, any training or specialized training needed, and to determine what relationships must be established.

**Leader Input:** Identify the CEO's intent, see gaps created by war-gaming to identify true requirements and the roles and expectations that support the CEO's intent.

Get what the CEO's vision is. As you continue planning, you will come to a point where you will war-game or determine the requirements and gaps identified in the planning effort. What are roles and expectations he sees? Who is going to do what?

**Insights:** Dashboard that provides holistic performance insights to track, drill, measure and links to crucial business metrics. Insights allow you to create multiple distribution ideas. You will gain insights into strategic direction, overall and specific changes to make, key positioning status, trends, distribution, requirement, readiness, technology, and relationship changes. Insights provide a sense of whether these areas are increasing or decreasing. You can get a general feel based upon either subjective measures or objective measures/metrics like the number of equipment on-hand or with no maintenance problems. Another example would be the trends in spending, resources used, and distribution hubs increasing or decreasing.

**Rules of Thumb:** Dashboard that provides general/standardized performance measures to track, drilldown, and act on crucial business metrics for your industry. Metrics on how long (time-distance) it will take to move supplies and equipment by air, seas, and land or the time it will take to contract the supplies and equipment or services. If you chose to obtain the supplies, equipment, or services from other countries, what is the Customs access time in days?  What are rules of thumb when determining force requirements?

In logistics, here are some Rules of Thumb to remember:

When planning, start with the Mission Command Structure that is needed to command and control the sustainment environment.  Normally, a Sustainment Brigade supported by a Combat Sustainment Support Battalion (CSSB) will be enough to do the job, although that can be modified to meet mission requirements. The Combat Sustainment Support Battalion (CSSB) operates the class I (subsistence) and water warehouse, supply support activity (SSA), class III (bulk petroleum) fuel farm, forward arming and refueling point, retail fuel point, ammunition supply point, and central receiving and shipping point (CRSP). This CSSB can be outfitted with whole units or composite teams called Forward Logistics Elements (FLE) that are tailored to meet the mission requirements for a Multi-Modal operations. Next you would look at the logistics functional areas that a FLE would execute and determine the number of people it would take to support the mission. A typical FLE can consist of between 9 – 45 people, with an average size of 20 people. It will generally be composed of the following functional areas:

FLE OIC/NCOIC (2 people)

Composite Supply Platoon:

CL I (Food) (2 people), CL I (Water) (1-3 people) (Field Feeding Teams)

CL III Coordinator (1 person) (Medium Truck Platoon w/maintenance)

CL III (Fuel) (2-4 people)

CL V (Munitions) (1-3 people) (Ordnance Support Maintenance Company)

Movement Control Team (Transportation) (2-5 people) (Heavy Equipment Transfer Platoon w/maintenance

Passenger Movement (2 people)

Maintenance Support Teams (CL IX parts requisitioned through GCSS-A (1-4 people) (Support Maintenance Platoon)

SAMs Clerk (1 person) (Human Resource/Postal/Gateway)

Finance Clerk (1 person)

Postal Clerk (1-2 people)

Medical (Area Support) (1-5 people)

Signal Clerks (3 people)

Mortuary Affairs (1 person)

Contractors/LOGCAP Team (as needed)

These would establish a logistics hub to manage things like Fuel points, Ammunition Supply Points, Supply Support Activity, and Retrograde Property Assistance Team (RPAT) yards.

Other logistics Rules of Thumbs:

- When establishing a supply support base, make sure you have 2-3 access points to be able to resupply the base.

- Rail and Ship is best for large movement of equipment.

- A double-line railroad, under wartime conditions, can move at least 50 or more trains (400 tons each) a day or 20K tons a day. A Two- lane road can do it at greater expense.

- A non-mechanized army requires only 15-30 pounds of supply per man per day. Every 1K tons of supply keeps 100K men in combat for a day. Even if supply below those levels, combat capability won't be reduced until over 33% of the requirement is denied. After that point 1 percent of the combat power is lost. Most units retain 33% of its combat power.

- Mechanized units require over 10 times as much supply per man. (Fuel key here 60% of movement, Ammunition 20% movement).

- Two places where logistics is key; wilderness (deserts, jungles, mountains, etc.) and small islands.

Still one must look at the Environment (It consists of conditions, circumstances, and influences).

**Key Inputs:** See levels of priority, domain, threat, power, and their significance and weights. The three levels that you will work with are on a strategic, operational, or tactical level. You will be trying to determine when a shift on one level impacts or shifts actions on another level. Domains are on a physical level, Cognitive level, or Moral level (Is it ethical?) What are threats? Are they a local, regional, or global threat? What impacts the elements of National Power – Political, Military, Economic, Social, Intellectual, and

Influence? What are the impacts of unknown or unanticipated inputs?

**Risk Development:** Two elements that should always be in the back of your mind when making decisions about acceptable risk: What is the risk to your mission and risk to people? Risks to mission can be major changes to lines of communications, lead-times for obtaining resources, available inventories on hand, or actions that increase or decrease requirements. Mal-positioned resources could also impact risk to mission. Risk to people could be the number of people available and their skillset. You can also look at ratios to determine if you have a good harmony in your capability versus a competitor. In the military, if one is on the defense, one would want a 1:3 ratio in operations to obtain success. If on the offense, one would want a 3:1 ratio. The next level to risk development is to determine when risk to mission shifts or exceeds the risk to force and then determine the mitigation strategies/actions that must be applied to achieve your desired effects/results.

**Metrics:** Identifies the key criteria when developing business metrics – determining when an action is efficient (uses the least number of steps) and effective (It works, regardless of steps/costs). Some Key Performance Indicators (KPI) are estimate of probability, relative or optimal value, trade-offs in time-cost, benefits, risks and opportunities, tensions and when are they in balance, price to cost, what are the significance, implications, and consequences, what is the priorities for essential information. To me one of the most critical metrics are what are the supply and movement rates.

**Mitigation Strategies:** Optional strategies you can use in scenario planning, course of action development, and war-gaming. Use scenario planning to look at the ideal scenario and what you would like to have happen, likely to happen or is more realistic, and then what could happen, but not likely to happen. Do you need to expand lines of communications, forecast requirements, preposition people and materials, prioritize and establish supply rates for supplies, establish manning levels, expand contracts, solicit support from other partners, and establish agreements that will allow for quicker and better understanding of operational requirements in determining when authorities /agreements are needed and how they will be used.

**Key Outputs:** Expected business effects/outputs that are the result of Business Intelligence Insights that lead to modified plans and planning. Other key outputs would be a good list of mission command size, how much money is needed, legal issues resolved, risks mitigated, and critical events determined. Still other key outputs could be that the main effort required is weighted, knowledge of the culminating point and line of diminishing returns, and knowledge of choke points and a validated synchronization of logistics in support of operations. Desired effects/outputs must be determined based on capabilities. Based upon the desired effects/outputs, you must identify priorities given the effects/outputs. You can also determine what do you maximize or minimize/highlight or hide. These outputs impact your reporting.

**Reporting:** Map visualizations maximize the ability to recognize the most important drivers that deliver efficient and effective outcomes. Standard reporting delivers the insight necessary to track metrics of performance and drive efficient and effective decision-making. You can report on the background (why you are taking action), Assessment (Who, What, and How and action is executed), and the Way Ahead (When, with time horizons 5 years, 1 year, Quarterly, Monthly, Weekly, and

Daily). You first **THINK** about what you expect to see, hear, and learn, **SEE** the current operating environment, **THINK** about what you have seen, heard, or learned, and then **DO**, take actions on what you now see, hear, and learn. This is the **THINK-SEE-THINK- DO** cycle. You can then summarize and report information that allows you to focus and act on the prioritized data that matters from most important to least, least controversial to most, negative to positive (always end on positive note), and then provide your recommendations and thoughts about multiple delivery options ensure you receive the insights needed to maximize strategic, operational, and tactical efficiencies. You will be able to unlock new insights to other critical areas of your business that will allow you to better understand and make sense of key drivers, themes, and talking points that influence each other to achieve the best outcome.

## Controlled Simplicity

### Control

Giving back control to customers is our top priority. You gain control when you solutions provide the flexibility and agility to meet your unique business needs. By combining your expertise and our user-friendly thinking model, you achieve new levels of controlling striated space for efficiency.

## Simplicity

More than ever, customers seek next level simplification - simplification in technology, distribution management, and in driving efficient order out of chaos. Simplicity starts with powerful yet flexible knowledge that makes it faster and easier for you to see real time solutions to problems. You will focus on the distribution systems rates and levels that increases efficiencies and thus reduce delays and increases customer satisfaction. Simplicity allows you to see when an operating environment shifts. These shifts are tied to information priorities that have been determined by the CEO or leadership as they look for indicators, pressures, triggers, decision points, and develop timelines.

Now, I've been retired from the military since 2008 and have had time to meditate on my 20-year experiences and will share my insight gained during peacetime and wartime on decision-making and how the Generals I knew thought that can be applied to Multi-Domain Triangulation.

Before I get to that, I want to share with you some coincidences that I found to be interesting about my life. The path that I have taken seemed familiar to me. Like I'd been there and done that before. I find coincidences, in places, in particularly interesting.

I've always had a connection with, it seems, General William T. Sherman, of the Union

Army. It seemed like I rode with him on his campaign through the South and my current military assignments lined-up with the places he
marched. It's like I could see eye to eye with him and had a sense of having known him always; in essence on the same path, road, truths, experiencing the beauties, errors, stars of life. One day, I sat back and thought, "this is weird".

General Sherman marched through Atlanta, Savannah, GA, and burned Columbia, SC. I was stationed in all three cities and now live in Columbia, SC. I was born 1964, one hundred years after General Sherman marched through Atlanta in 1864. There seems to be a connection with 100 years rebirth in reincarnation circles/beliefs. Not only that, my relatives on my mother's side last name is Sherman; although my relatives on my father's side last name is Davis. The first crush I had on girl had the last name of Lee. So being around Generals seemed normal to me because it seemed to be in my DNA.

So being around the select group of people who have "real power" who are the "go to" individuals who make it things happen seem to be normal. Again, I witnessed this during my military career, when the U.S. Army would bring in a select group of people, usually Generals, to manage a military campaign. You could call them the "Dream Team". This Dream Team is in all successful organizations and must be searched out when you encounter each pillar that supports the Power Hub discussed in earlier chapters of this book.

Prior to and during the Iraq War, I had the opportunity to brief and sit in a room of Generals to discuss plans. The things that I noticed about how they make decisions are amazing. They are indeed rare individuals, with each having a singularity of focus based on their background experiences. Traits that I noted about them, they were an uncommon group that displayed imagination, instinct, calm, speaking ability, charismatic, with physical size, and daring in their attitude. They had an almost poetic way of thinking.

Each had an organizational mind and just seemed brilliant in determining how to get results from chaos by having a process to *filter incoming information.*

Over my career, I've been blessed to work with and shook hands with brilliant Generals with names such as Christianson, Shelton, Thurmond, Franks, Wallace, Jones, and many others. Their unique ability and art at asking questions of others and evaluate the response were the key underpinnings to their strength. They also had a birds-eye view of organizational structures, systems, and processes and how they work on different levels to achieve strategic, operational, and tactical success.

They could see current disposition and anticipate future needs in an ever-flowing risky environment. They did this by looking for impressions, indicators, and deploying sensors within the environment to see the power within it to address top-tier problems even in an asymmetric environment.

To have power or the ability to influence and control things to get things done, you must know what power is, it's pillars of support and the functions within each, such as the people who work there and their certifications/training levels, their reach or influence, the equipment or tools that they use, the systems they put together to produce output, and the processes used to make the system work. You should focus on the costs, savings, and efficiencies gained.

Now here is the key to opening the door to understanding life by using what I call Exponential Thinking applied to obstacles that you face in your life to filter incoming information from all sources like the Generals did.
Discovering the truth, the secret to understanding Exponential Thinking is this:

The ability to think and act faster than the competition using sensors and sharper networks.

To understand exponentially increasing information, you must decrease your thinking by assigning color codes to what the information means to you, and then determine the centers of gravity of the codes from your known position or point, or what I sometimes call; your X spot.

X is everywhere apparent, but nowhere stated directly.

You have often seen X and heard of X when you were shown a treasure map with a dotted line and arrow that lead to a spot on the map that had the X on it.

Most of us, say that the X is where the treasure is buried.

We often overlook the X; while focusing on the buried treasure. We even say "X marks the spot".

The X is the secret of secrets. Knowing X determines the worth, authorities, and rewards that lead to strategic geometry and wisdom.

You have seen a football game, and when someone wants to show how a play develops, they use X's and O's. We pay attention to the X's and O's, but don't see the secret, which is being shown right before us.

In mathematics, we say, "solve for X". Now, X is the secret to understanding

Exponential Thinking that will allow you to understand what to do with the

 an ever-increasing amount of news and information that is coming at you.

X stands for the Roman number ten.  In numbers, it is represented as 10.

Our numbering system is based on ten.

Computers communicate using 1 and 0.

They use a binary code of $10^7$, $10^6$, $10^5$, $10^4$, $10^3$, $10^2$, $10^1$, $10^0$.  So you get     $10^1$ x 1 = 10, $10^2$ = 100, $10^3$ = 1,000, and so forth.

For every sequence, you get 10 times the result.

It gets away from the linear way we think and provides information 10 times for every sequence or count.

To keep up with the information coming at you, we've discovered that you must use the following three sequences:

Sequence 1: Reduce information coming at you to its *root or basic name*. Further, reduce the basic name using substrings. For example, prosperity, has a root name of prospering, a substring to that would be *pro* and *sper.* You can then add a pre-fix or suffix to the word to extend or create additional word meanings like prosper*ed,* prosper*ing, etc.* Adding -ed, -er, -ing, -ly allows you to expand into greater meaning/ language.

Using substrings allow you to reduce the information down to its sub-elements. At the substring level, you can begin to attach meaning to words like an incomplete puzzle. You simply begin to see each letter as an indicator of the word, sentence, or paragraph that is about to come.

It is also at this level that you will start to attach a value to what the letter, words "is" and what it "does". Is it relevant to what you are imagining or desiring?

Once you get its meaning, you move on to sequence 2.

Sequence 2: You assign a color to the word. The color represents whether the word represents a threat or friendly results for you. If you perceive the word as a threat, you use the color red. If you perceive it as friendly, you use green. If you perceive it as neutral, use yellow.

Assigning a color to words, allows you to see threats quicker. As you know, one of the first things the eye notices when walking into a room is color. It then tries to determine the shape, so the next tool you can use it the element of line/shape. Your eye will try to determine the pattern if one is discernible.

Now colors can be of a Hue, Intensity, or Value. This can be shown if the color is determined to be a hot or cold, warm or cool, color. This can be shown by different shades or tints.

The line element can be shown as horizontal, vertical, diagonal, or curvilinear. Typically, Horizontal reveals width and side-to-side movement, vertical lines reveal height or up and down movement, diagonal reveals angle or dynamic interest, and curvilinear reveals tension.

Being able to see the line or shape and color will allow you to determine whether what you are seeing is friendly or not.

What you are looking for is what in graphic design we call harmony or balance. You are looking for a fluid flow of thought.

When you see something in balance, it means that you have the capability to meet whatever information is coming at you. If you see something that is out of balance and is represented by the color "red" then, you know that you will automatically pay attention to it because it is not friendly.

You would then use the line element to determine if it is heading directly at you or from an angle.

All of this takes place in seconds or less to the Sharper Thinker.

What you are doing is using the nature or built in the way your body is designed to recognize things. It is one of the driving factors that has to allow humans to continue to exist, the survival instinct.

Plus you are using what you desire and your ability to be curious about things or your curiosity to imagine what information is coming at you. (strategic foresight)

These factors determine your perception of what you see or make suggestions of what might be in the near future.

Finally, Sequence 3: Use Center of Gravity concepts to place the colors on a *mental map*.

Take the colors and picture them in your mind as if they are on a map. You will put yourself in the spot shown in the center of the X.

There must be a move to develop your thinking using the concept of center of gravity. You have to determine your decision points and vulnerabilities in order to solve the current problems and protect yourself from a large amount of information that is being generated. Again, Claude Von Clausewitz felt that center of gravity is the concentration of "hub" of power. From that point or position, place all of the "red" colors, then the "yellow" colors, and finally, the "green" colors.

This will reveal to you the threats that the incoming information may have on you.

Use your curiosity or imagination at this time to allow you to read and judge the focal point and how colors/things are categorized or grouped around the point.

It will allow you to ask if there is a natural balance of resources? What is the weight of the various components and will the foundations support them?

You can use these three sequences for they are the secret master key to exponential thinking. This process will allow you to see things coming sooner and give you some reaction time that others who are not using this process will not have.

It is the seed to your success.

In every word is the seed to its mastery. Information has within it the seeds of success. We just have to use this substring, color-coded, and center of gravity process to reach success.

Now that you know what the X is, you must start using it today. You have taken the road less traveled.

That road is to be consciously taken until it becomes an unconscious habit.

This must be done daily.

What you see reflected will then create in you the feelings and skills that you need and desire to become a more confident person.

It is not an easy road to follow, because most people naturally don't do it.

So consciously make it a point to think this way until you can do it without thinking and you will experience much success in becoming a master of filtering information using these steps to concentrated strategic thinking:

**Sequence 1:** You first **Ask** the most important questions at all times…**Am I doing the right thing, things right, and where are the center or pillar, essential meaning, and purpose of what I'm seeing**?

**Sequence 2: Seek** the many connections/relationships and different ways (perspectives) by looking around you, paying attention to what you see, know, and do now and expect to see, know, do to influence the future.

**Sequence 3: Know:** Seeing the meaning of places, people, and things while grasping the grand drama requires imagination based on seeing levels and expectations. Wisdom will be developed by instinctively judging what right action to take, based on knowledge, insight, experience, common sense, and understanding to see things differently, more broadly, and deeply.

You must **MEASURE** all that you do. That is, you must be sure of what actions to take because you have calculated and then can anticipate the outcome. Be able to see the extreme ends of a problem or question and then ask if time is a critical factor in solving or answering it. Determine the worth, authorities, and rewards.

Listen for the subtle connections that are shown by pain levels, desire, honor, and any new information that comes to mind and then act on it until you meet with success.

Dinosaurs have long disappeared from the Earth, but the butterfly remains. What is the secret to its ability to endure? I believe that now that you understand and apply the triggers and indicator tools presented in this book, you can live a long successful life no matter the change that is around you.

I know that after reading this eye-opening, hands-on book, you now know how to integrate and control any environment by learning how to use concentrated, guided thinking to sense how to increase the velocity of resources across time and space, in the right amount, at the right place, to identify tradeoffs and risks in chaotic environments.   Yes, the eye is the secret of it all, because the eye sees what's in it range.  It sees nothing or everything.  You also will use the contents of this book as a guide to use when you need to make course corrections as you navigate by using sensors to help transform objective foundations of thought; which is based on mathematics like calculus and geometry. Now, you will be able to analyze and sort out what's important and interesting as you put things into context, see new insights, and anticipate trends. You finally see that that center of gravity is a continuous process throughout events and that center of gravity can change during the course of an event and may not be apparent or readily discernible.

This book you've read provided insights and original ideas for you as a sharper thinker on how to be a master intellect and creative genius. These underpinning tools will integrate and control any environment by guiding your thinking to sense how to increase the velocity of resources across time and space in the right amount at the right place while reducing risks and embarrassing delays.

This book has provided comprehensive and sound underpinning tools and now you have them; for they lead to the answers to how to think exponentially when trying to sense and determine what's important now and in the future that will lead to less redundancies and risk and produce greater successes as you think from a longer and sharper perspective. You can now began creatively seizing the initiative with awareness, foresight, timing, and imagination.

Still further, this comprehensive book you have read indeed provided insights for mastering the art of Multi-Domain Triangulation by using a strategy of layered/relational networked geometry/spatial projection of forces and fluid flow distribution that allows exponential growth in flexibility, precision, and coordination to anticipate and be imaginative in any environment.

Now, the driving theme for this book is the question, **how to leverage Multi-Domain Triangulation at the cutting-edge of**

**success?** We answered that question in a profound way in this book. Multi-Domain Triangulation consists of three areas that will be discussed throughout this book:

(1)     Think and Feel Outside-the-Box in the face of Battle

(2)     Use Risk-taking on a Breath-taking scale based on priorities

(3)     Master of time, space, and mass (concentration)

The answer to the driving theme for this book is that yes, width always at the expense of knowing processes and underpinnings, and the good news is that you can integrate and control any environment by using your imagination to guide your thinking, sensing how to increase the velocity of resources across time and space in the right amount at the right place.

You are now thinking at a triangulated level…but remember and know this secret, life is an art, strategy and timing is key to success in life, and there is always another level.

# ABOUT THE AUTHOR

He's known as one of the world's unified thinkers and founder of a breakthrough thinking method called Context Thinking. He is also the founder of *The Black Chair Series*.

A 10-year veteran of the context thinking field, Joseph Graham is unique among experts as the man who's actually developed and executed the day-to-day thinking strategies.

Today, he's the #1 best selling author of *Master The Art of Context*

*Thinking, The 11 Golden Principles of Context Thinking, The Game of Life and Its Lessons, Thinking Quadrant: How to Think on Your Feet Even When You're Sitting, Blockchain Thinking, Master of the Situation*, and many others, published worldwide.

Other information can be found at http://jgrahamenterprises.wixsite.com/one pagebooks

**Check out our newest product offering: "One Page Books".** We help you save time by providing you exactly what you need to answer questions at the right time. You can subscribe starting at $1 per month. You get a minimum of 12 great books per year.

Made in the USA
Las Vegas, NV
10 October 2023

78883399R10085